CHOSEN
YOUR JOURNEY TOWARD CONFIRMATION

SPONSOR'S GUIDE

Colin & Aimee MacIver

This Sponsor's Guide is a component of the
Chosen: Your Journey Toward Confirmation program.
General Editors: Chris Stefanick and Ron Bolster

ASCENSION

West Chester, Pennsylvania

Ascension
Post Office Box 1990
West Chester, PA 19380
1-800-376-0520
ascensionpress.com

Cover Design: Devin Schadt

Printed in the United States of America

ISBN: 978-1-935940-55-5

Contents

Welcome! You have been invited to sponsor a candidate for Confirmation, an invitation of great honor and responsibility. A "sponsor" is not just an honorary title; it is a calling. Your candidate has identified you as a living witness of faith in Jesus Christ and his Church. With this honor comes the responsibility to guide and support your candidate as he or she prepares for the Sacrament of Confirmation and beyond. You are called to be a Christian witness, friend, prayer warrior, and ally to your candidate for the rest of your life.

You may have questions and perhaps even some hesitations about your role as sponsor. This guide will help you become an effective sponsor by renewing and encouraging your personal growth in Catholic Faith and life. This Sponsor's Guide includes practical ideas for engaging your candidate and provides clear answers to questions that are often asked—by teens and adults—about the fundamentals of the Catholic Faith.

The most important and effective part of your sponsorship is prayer. May the Holy Spirit inspire and encourage you as you accompany your candidate on the journey to the fullness of life in Christ.

Part 1

An Introduction to Becoming a Confirmation Sponsor

"The sponsor is to take care that the confirmed person behaves as a true witness of Christ ..."

–*Code of Canon Law* 892

Chapter 1

What Is Confirmation?

Confirmation is a sacramental outpouring of the Holy Spirit that leaves a permanent imprint on the soul, completes Christian initiation, and empowers us to be witnesses to Christ (see CCC 1302–1305).

Many people mistakenly see Confirmation as a teen's "graduation" from religious education, as merely a cultural passage into maturity, or as an opportunity to choose whether or not to remain Catholic. None of these views is consistent with the teaching of the Church on this powerful sacrament. Confirmation is not merely a symbolic ceremony or a rite of passage. While it is true that a candidate chooses whether to receive the Sacrament of Confirmation and, with the reception of the sacrament, takes a step toward maturity (and, yes, mandatory catechism classes often do come to an end), none of these facts captures the heart of the meaning of the Sacrament of Confirmation.

What happens at Confirmation?

As with every sacrament, Confirmation does not merely symbolize a spiritual reality—it actually effects what it signifies. In Confirmation, our senses are fully engaged: We see the bishop's hand raise in anointing. The candidate feels and smells the *sacred chrism*, or sacramental oil, and hears the bishop proclaim, "Be sealed with the Gift of the Holy Spirit."

What we physically see, hear, feel, and smell in Confirmation is an anointing, a sealing with the Holy Spirit. These visible elements are not merely symbolic: Working through what is visible and sensory, the same Holy Spirit who was poured out upon the apostles at Pentecost makes a permanent mark on the newly confirmed person's soul.

When the Holy Spirit descended upon the apostles as they prayed together at Pentecost (see Acts 1–2), the effects of this miracle were immediately apparent. The apostles proclaimed their faith fearlessly. The sacramental presence of the Holy Spirit in their souls emboldened them to speak the truth. The *Catechism of the Catholic Church* lists five effects of Confirmation (see CCC 1303):

- It affirms our identity as children of God ("divine filiation").

- It unites us more firmly to Christ.

- It increases in us the Gifts of the Holy Spirit.

- It strengthens our bond with the Church.

- It strengthens us to spread and defend the Faith by our words and actions, to be fearless witnesses to Christ and the power of the cross.

What is the relationship between Confirmation and Baptism?

Confirmation "completes" the graces we received at Baptism (see CCC 1304), when we became adopted sons and daughters of God. Confirmation *confirms* that we are part of God's family and leads us to focus on what we have been called to do as children of God: to be living witnesses of God's love in the world.

In Confirmation, we receive the power to make a stand for Christ and his Church, as well as special gifts to help us serve God and the Church in particular ways. Through the sacrament, we are also "sealed" for God; our bond with him, as well as with the whole family of God, is strengthened. All these graces help us to shift our focus from interior formation (which began at Baptism) to exterior *proclamation,* giving us courage to witness to the Faith in our words and actions (see CCC 1305). Confirmation is sometimes called "the sacrament of the martyrs" because the word *martyr* derives from the Greek word meaning "witness." The martyrs witnessed to the truth of the gospel—no matter what the cost.

Does the Holy Spirit give everyone gifts at Confirmation?

Many people think, "I was confirmed ... and none of *that* happened to me." This seeming disconnect between the Church's teaching on Confirmation and people's personal experiences of it reveals an important truth about the sacraments: *While sacramental grace can work powerfully, we must be ready to receive the gifts the Spirit wants to give us.*

This reality is clear in Jesus' parable of the sower (Mark 4:1-20): Seed is scattered in many places, but it flourishes only in the right kind of soil.

What is my primary role as a Confirmation sponsor?

A sponsor has three primary roles: (1) to assist the candidate in preparing for Confirmation, (2) to present the candidate for Confirmation, and (3) to help the confirmed person to live out his or her Christian faith fully. There are several ways you can help your candidate.

Share your own experiences. Lead him or her closer to Christ by telling your candidate about your own spiritual journey.

Spend time talking and listening. Help your candidate grow in understanding and acceptance of Christ and the teachings of his Church. (This book will help you.)

Pray for your candidate regularly. Pray that he or she will not only come to know *about* the Faith, but also will encounter Christ while preparing to receive the sacrament. As a sponsor, commit to lifting your candidate up in prayer every day.

Encourage him or her to grow in virtue and to set aside any habits that would prevent his or her soul from being fully open and ready to receive all the gifts God wants to give him or her through the Sacrament of Confirmation.

How does the Chosen *program work to prepare my candidate for Confirmation?*

Chosen will lead your candidate on a journey through the Catholic Faith in all its richness and vitality. Over the course of twenty-four engaging and powerful lessons, your candidate will not only learn about the Faith, but will be invited to experience a *personal encounter with Jesus Christ.* Using a combination of videos, workbook material, and group discussions, the goal of the *Chosen* program is to win over the hearts of youth at this critical time in their lives and to keep them firmly planted in the faith community of the Church.

The video presentations in this program feature some of the top youth ministers in the Church today and have been filmed on location throughout the country and internationally. A dynamic and engaging workbook is used throughout the program and contains at-home pages and activities that are an essential part of the *Chosen* learning experience.

Part 2 of this Sponsor's Guide ("Four Important Conversations to Have with Your Candidate") provides a list of the lessons as well as "Conversation Starters"—questions you can ask your candidate to engage and encourage him or her during this exciting journey.

A Sacrament Is:

Effective. A sacrament actually brings into existence the spiritual reality it symbolizes.

Outward. A sacrament appeals to our senses: You can see, hear, touch, smell, and sometimes even taste a sacrament.

From Christ. The sacraments are Christ's idea, not ours.

A source of grace. Sacraments give grace, the free gift of God's own life.

Given to us through the Church. The Church hands on and celebrates what Christ instituted.

Chapter 2

What Is a Sponsor?

What was your first reaction when you were invited to be a Confirmation sponsor? Were you excited? Nervous? Did you wonder if you had what it takes to do the job well?

Do not be afraid. You do not need a doctorate in theology for this job. We have already touched upon some of the things you can do to make sure your candidate is ready. In addition, you may want to use this opportunity to take a look at the *Catechism* and other Catholic resources to refresh your own knowledge of the Faith. As you find answers to your own questions, you will be better able to guide your candidate to legitimate sources of Catholic teaching.

In a real sense, it is easier now than at any other time in history to know precisely what the Church teaches and why. The *Catechism of the Catholic Church* is a great treasury of Catholic teachings. In addition, there are many reliable resources to help you—including this Sponsor's Guide!

What qualifies someone to be a Confirmation sponsor?

A sponsor must have the following qualifications:

1) be a Catholic who is at least sixteen years old.[1]

2) have received the Sacrament of Confirmation.

---

[1]   "... unless the diocesan bishop has established another age, or the pastor or minister has granted an exception for a just cause" (*Code of Canon Law* 874).

3) be a person who leads "a life of faith in keeping with the function to be taken on."[2]

4) not be a parent of the candidate.

In short, a sponsor should be a fully initiated Catholic who is faithful to Christ and his Church. Because of the deep connection between the two sacraments, the Church recommends that the candidate's baptismal godparents be considered as Confirmation sponsors.[3]

Have Any Photos of Your Confirmation?

If so, consider sharing them with your candidate as a way of starting a personal conversation with him or her about the sacrament.

What if I am not sure I have what it takes to be a good sponsor?

If you feel spiritually inadequate to be a Confirmation sponsor, consider this as an invitation from God to grow in your own faith. He loves you, after all. If something glaring has been separating you from God, maybe now is the time to bring that to Confession. Your candidate sees something spiritually admirable in you—something in you that inspires him or her in the Catholic Faith. Set aside any self-doubt, and consider that

---

[2]   *Code of Canon Law* 874.
[3]   *Code of Canon Law* 893.

God may be calling you to this role for the sake of examining your own heart as well as guiding your candidate.

Nothing promotes personal growth like forgetting ourselves and turning toward another. The best way to be a good sponsor is to pray often for your candidate and to keep your own eyes fixed on Jesus. Do not be afraid if you are not perfect. It is often said, "The Church is not a museum of saints, but a hospital for sinners."

What role do I play before, during, and after the sacramental rite?

Your most important job as a sponsor is to be a "spiritual help" to your candidate: "The sponsor is to take care that the confirmed person behaves as a true witness of Christ and faithfully fulfills the obligations inherent in this sacrament."[4] So your primary responsibility is to ensure that your candidate is genuinely ready to receive the Sacrament of Confirmation and to live out the mission that comes with it.

---

[4]   *Code of Canon Law* 892.

Start Praying Now!

Beginning today, commit to some small daily act of prayer, service, or sacrifice for your candidate, and record what you do each day in a journal. At Confirmation, give the journal to your candidate as a keepsake.

Make a Date!

If possible, invite your candidate to go to Confession with you. Even if it has been awhile, you can give yourself a "faith lift" by going to Confession this week. Most parishes make Confession available at least once a week. See your parish bulletin or contact the parish office for the Confession schedule.

How to ensure this readiness is a broad question that this guide will explore. Briefly, however, your role is to:

- Discuss with your candidate the content of the Catholic Faith.

- Provide a "sounding board" for your candidate to talk about his or her spiritual life, habits, hopes, fears, and struggles.

- Be a good example of the Christian life to your candidate.

- Pray with and for your candidate.

What if I am unable to spend time with my candidate before his or her Confirmation day?

Technology can be very helpful to connect you with your candidate. As a young person, your candidate probably has a smart phone, sends text messages, and uses social media on a daily basis. Take advantage of these media sources to communicate with him or her, even if your schedule requires such contacts to be brief.

A simple "I am praying for you today" text message can be a powerful reminder that you take your sponsorship seriously. This signals your candidate that you take him or her seriously—which is the key to communicating with teenagers.

Post a link to the upcoming Sunday's readings in a private message on your candidate's social media account (e.g., Facebook, Twitter, or Instagram), along with a thought-provoking question about the readings or a few words of your own reflection on them. Do not overlook more traditional but very meaningful communication methods—a short letter or postcard with an inspirational or encouraging message is unusual enough to make a big impact.

Why do these things? Such simple acts are both personal and targeted specifically at your candidate. Nearly all teenagers need this kind of personal interaction, and they will eagerly respond to it. Because you are the candidate's chosen sponsor (and not a parent, teacher, or some other authority figure), your candidate is less likely to resist or shrug off this kind of outreach from you. You have the potential to make a significant impact at this time in your candidate's life.

Throughout this book, you will find outreach ideas to consider and adapt to fit the needs of your particular candidate.

Follow the Pope!

For some bite-sized papal commentary to share and discuss with your candidate, follow the Holy Father on Twitter. His handle is @pontifex. He is currently re-tweeted more than any other world leader.

What will I need to do or say at the Confirmation ceremony? What should I say to the bishop?

A sponsor's part of the sacramental rite is simple. You and your candidate will process to the altar in a line similar to a Communion line with the other sponsors and candidates. If you receive no specific instructions about what to say ahead of time, when your candidate gets to the front of the line, simply place your right hand on your candidate's right shoulder and say, "Your Excellency (or "Your Eminence," if the bishop is a cardinal), "I present *[name of the patron saint your candidate has chosen, or baptismal name if no saint was chosen]*." (Note: If the confirming bishop takes the lead and asks the candidate directly what his or her name is, there is no need for you to say anything.)

If you meet the bishop at a reception or before the ceremony, and the more formal greeting ("Your Excellency" or "Your Eminence") slips your mind, do not panic. Most bishops are fine with simply being addressed by their title: "bishop," "archbishop," or "cardinal."

Questions? Get the Right Answers!

The United States Conference of Catholic Bishops (USCCB) offers an online *Catechism of the Catholic Church* (CCC), which can be searched by topic or term. Visit usccb.org.

What do I need to do after my candidate has been confirmed?

After your candidate has received the Sacrament of Confirmation, your role as an encouraging mentor of faith continues. Obviously, each situation allows for different levels of ongoing contact, but it is fitting to check in often with your candidate. Continue encouraging him or her in the life of faith. As best you can, send a clear message that Confirmation was not a "graduation" from religious education but a fuller initiation into the Christian Faith. Developing consistent communication prior to Confirmation will be helpful in continuing the relationship with your candidate.

Confession: What If I Do Not Remember the Words?

Do not worry—the priest will be more than happy to lead you through each step. Believe it or not, there are apps for that. If you have a smart phone, search your app store for the word "confession" to be directed to various options. You can also use this simple Act of Contrition:

My God, I am sorry for my sins with all my heart. In choosing to do wrong and failing to do good, I have sinned against you whom I should love above all things.

I firmly intend, with your help, to do penance, to sin no more, and to avoid whatever leads me to sin.

Our Savior, Jesus Christ, suffered and died for us.

In his name, my God, have mercy. Amen.

Chapter 3

How Can I Help My Candidate Prepare for the Sacrament?

Two of the most important things you can do to help your Confirmation candidate prepare for the sacrament are (1) be personally committed to prayer and (2) impress upon your candidate, by word and example, the importance of participating in the sacramental life of the Church. The principal way we participate in the church's sacramental life is through regular reception of the Eucharist and the Sacrament of Reconciliation.

Sadly, many Catholics do not attend Sunday Mass, which is the most vital, basic element in the life of faith. Irregular commitment to weekly Sunday Mass has many serious consequences for one's "spiritual health." By your own example, you can help to ensure that these two sacraments become an active and habitual part of your candidate's Catholic life.

Why is going to Mass every week so important?

As Catholics, we are called to "conscious, active, and fruitful participation" (see CCC 1071) in weekly Sunday Mass. The "Sunday Eucharist is the foundation and confirmation of all Christian practice" (CCC 2181). By making Mass a priority, we observe the third commandment to "Remember the Sabbath day, to keep it holy" (Exodus 20:8) as well as Jesus' command to "do this in remembrance of me" (Luke 22:19). To fail to meet

Go to Mass!

A key goal of sponsorship is to energize and encourage your candidate's participation in Mass. Invite your candidate to attend Mass with you. If this is not possible, take advantage of texting and social media to encourage your candidate to attend Mass and to share your thoughts about the homily or weekly Scripture readings.

this serious obligation is to damage our relationship with God and put our spiritual well-being at risk.

Similarly, when we miss Mass, we "starve" ourselves spiritually. When we receive Jesus in the Eucharist, we experience "the source and summit" (CCC 1324) of our Catholic Faith and receive an infusion of Jesus' divine life.[5] To miss Mass, then, is to deny ourselves the immeasurable grace of receiving him in Communion. At Mass, Jesus offers himself to us: Gathering our works, joys, and sufferings, he transforms them in the most powerful way. What could possibly be more important?

While the reality of the Eucharist is hidden under the appearance of bread and wine, St. Thomas Aquinas reminds us in his traditional benediction hymn *Tantum Ergo:* "What is hidden to our senses, we grasp with the help of faith."

---

[5]   Second Vatican Council, *Lumen Gentium* II.

Why is going to Confession an important part of the Christian life?

In the Sacrament of Reconciliation, we confess our sins to God through the priest, who has been given the authority to act *in persona Christi,* i.e., with the very authority of Christ himself (see CCC 1548). In the Sacrament of Reconciliation, the priest lends his face, hands, and voice to Christ so that we may have the powerful sensory experience of seeing and hearing, in the words of absolution, that our sins have been forgiven, and that our relationship with Christ and the Church has been restored.

By giving his apostles the power to forgive sins (see John 20:21-23), Christ instituted the Sacrament of Reconciliation as a way to heal and restore the damage caused by sin. Remember that the seal of Confession is absolute. The Church binds the priest to absolute secrecy about any sins revealed to him in Confession even under the threat of imprisonment, physical injury, or death. A priest who breaks the sacramental seal incurs an automatic excommunication.[6]

Perhaps you have not been to Confession in a while. Consider your sponsorship as an occasion for your spiritual growth. What an authentic witness to your candidate it is when you examine your own heart, trust Jesus, and seek true freedom! There is no more powerful way to give your candidate the strength and courage to do the same.

---

6   See *Code of Canon Law* 1388.

Gift Idea

At the beginning of the formation process, give your candidate a rosary, and invite him or her to pray the Rosary with you every week leading up to Confirmation. If you cannot meet weekly, plan to pray the Rosary at the same time each week. Be sure to follow up with a "reminder" call or text to let your candidate know you remembered him or her.

What if I am uncomfortable praying aloud? Do I still need to pray with my candidate?

We tend to overcomplicate prayer. St. Thérèse of Lisieux tells us that prayer is "a simple look turned toward heaven" (CCC 2558).[7]

There are many traditional prayers and devotions that can turn you toward heaven. You and your candidate may participate in a particular devotion together, such as praying the Rosary or a novena to the candidate's chosen patron saint, attending a prayer group, or visiting a Eucharistic Adoration chapel. It is also powerful just to talk to Jesus from your heart with your candidate, thanking God for his blessings and asking him for whatever you need.[8]

If you are not able to do these prayers or devotions together due to distance or other conflicts, you and your candidate could agree to cultivate the same "prayer habit"—like offering a decade of the Rosary for each other on Fridays, for example—

---

[7] St. Thérèse of Lisieux, *Manuscrits autobiographiques,* C 25r.
[8] See page 70 for directions on how to pray the Rosary.

as a form of spiritual solidarity. You can also fast, offering up little sacrifices, like dessert, for your candidate. Fasting is the practice of abstaining from certain foods, or even all food, for a period of time as a way to "deny yourself and take up your cross" (Matthew 16:24). Fasting can help you to pray with greater intentionality and to focus more on God.

How do I talk to a teenager about faith, Jesus, and moral issues?

First, take heart. Your candidate has chosen you because he or she admires you and holds you in regard. As a sponsor, you have a distinct advantage over any other authority figure—you were personally *chosen* by your candidate.

Any communication with teenagers must be honest above all else. Despite the fact that their own behavior is often unpredictable and inconsistent, teenagers have a keen sense of whether or not adults believe what they say. They want to be treated as increasingly mature and independent young adults, not as children.

Three Rules for Sharing

1. Do not glorify sinful behavior or encourage experimentation.
2. Give only as much detail as is needed to make your point.
3. Be straightforward, honest, and encouraging.

Here are some things to keep in mind as you talk with your candidate:

1. *Avoid presenting yourself as an expert or as someone who never makes mistakes.* Draw from your own life to illustrate a point or emphasize an aspect of faith. (Show appropriate discretion, and avoid giving "license" to undesirable behaviors. It is OK, and often advisable, to be vague when talking about your own faults with a teenager.) Your role is simply to use your own honest experiences to guide him or her.

In deciding whether to share a particular story, consider carefully how much detail is needed to make a particular point. Sponsors and others who work with teens are often drawn to share about their personal experiences in order to establish credibility and to relate to the struggles common to teens. This can be helpful, if done prudently; damaging, if done imprudently. Ask God to give you the wisdom to know what to share. Strive to imitate St. Augustine, whose *Confessions* drew from his own experiences, good and bad, to point readers to the truths of the Catholic Faith.

Sponsorship in the Digital Age

Are you connected with your candidate on Facebook or Twitter? How much does your candidate use text messaging? Use Facebook wall posts, tweets, and texts to encourage your candidate along the way.

2. Listen for the "question behind the question." If your candidate asks you a difficult question, seek to discover what he or she is really getting at. Teens often ask a particular question, but there is really a deeper issue they are trying to understand.

3. Be sure you understand the question before responding. You may want to repeat your candidate's question before answering it, in order to be sure you understand what he or she is asking. As much as possible, talk to your candidate honestly and directly; do not water down the truth. Teenagers appreciate honesty, even if they are not yet fully mature and able to deal with the truth of your answer.

4. Whenever possible, find a point of affirmation or agreement to build upon. Avoid conversation-ending statements such as, "That is just how it is," or, "You must believe it because that is what the Church teaches." Affirm what is good in your candidate's opinions—even if it is just to praise his or her willingness to grapple with hard questions. For instance, if you are asked about why priests are celibate when we are all called to love, you may say something like, "You are right—*everyone* has a need for love, not just those who are married. And yet, Jesus and many of the saints never married—how did they experience love? Let's talk about it."

Teenagers sometimes ask questions that may seem crude or silly, but you should assume that each question is sincere and that the teenager may not have learned yet how to express themselves more delicately. More than anything else, teenagers want to be taken seriously. These gestures of respect will help your candidate feel more open and will foster genuine conversation.

What if my candidate questions basic Catholic teachings, such as whether God exists?

First, pray for the gift of faith for your candidate, and share the life of faith with your candidate—praying, encouraging, and engaging in acts of service with him or her. Christianity is not a science to figure out, but a life to live. When lived well, many questions disappear. And good answers to theological questions do not necessarily translate to faith. Faith is about building a relationship with God.

That said, never gloss over a question. Questions can be very important in helping your candidate develop a genuine, mature faith. St. Anselm, a doctor of the Church, gave us a clear formula for the relationship between faith and questioning: "Faith seeking understanding." When our faith is stirred up, we naturally ask questions and want to know more.[9]

As questions are sparked in the heart and mind of your candidate, you can be a reliable guide to the truth by seeking answers from the *Catechism,* Scripture, and other trustworthy sources. To help you prepare for your candidate's questions, this book includes an outline of formation topics covered in the *Chosen* program (Part 2, "Four Important Conversations to Have with Your Candidate"), as well some of the questions most commonly asked by Catholics (Part 3, "Top Ten Catholic Questions").

---

[9] Similarly, if there are certain aspects of Church teaching that you find difficult to accept, pray for the gift of faith for yourself. Then, use your time as a Confirmation sponsor to learn more about this subject from reliable Catholic sources, such as the *Catechism,* and pray for discernment. In this way, you will become a living witness to the importance of continuing to learn and grow in the Faith, even in adulthood.

Personal Testimony

What has Jesus done for you? The Faith is most effectively spread not by experts but by witnesses. Sharing the good things God is doing in your personal life will encourage your candidate to do the same.

More Ideas for Sponsorship in the Digital Age

- *Text a daily or weekly Scripture verse* for your candidate to reflect upon.

- *Post spiritually encouraging notes or links* on your candidate's social media accounts.

- *Send brief postcards or e-cards* to your candidate before a big game or important test.

- *Become "pen pals"* via email or Facebook messages. Ask your candidate about his or her struggles, curiosities, questions, anxieties, worries, or hopes, and respond in writing.

- *Skype or text before Sunday Mass* and talk for a few minutes about the upcoming readings.

- *Don't give up!* Teenagers do not always reveal how a particular outreach effort touches them. Even if you do not observe a positive response, any genuinely loving outreach will make a powerful impression on your candidate.

Four Important Conversations to Have with Your Candidate

"Empower me, Jesus, to be a living witness to you,
especially to the candidate you have entrusted to me."

Your Candidate's *Chosen* Journey

In the *Chosen* program, the three phases of the catechumenate (sacramental preparation) are expressed in the organization and structure of the program, following this classic Scripture passage: "Jesus said to him, 'I am the way, and the truth, and the life; no one comes to the Father, but by me'" (John 14:6). In *Chosen,* we discover that Jesus is ...

- **The Way** (pre-catechumenate, or "discovering" the Faith)

- **The Truth** (catechumenate, or "learning" the Faith)

- **The Life** (purification and enlightenment, or "living" the Faith)

Following the celebration of the sacrament is a fourth phase, called *mystagogy.* In this phase, the newly initiated Christian is immersed in the life of the Christian community. Once your candidate has been confirmed, encourage him or her to seek out and get involved in a local parish-based youth group in order to continue his or her spiritual journey.

Use the *Chosen* program as a way of tracking your candidate's spiritual progress and as a source for discussion: "What did your class cover this week? What part was most interesting? What were the group discussions like?" By tracking along with the lesson titles listed on the following pages, you can know when to engage your candidate in conversations on particular topics.

Supporting and Encouraging Your Candidate

This section of the Sponsor's Guide includes prayers, reflections, and conversation starters that you can use in a variety of ways, both on your own and with your candidate, to support him or her in preparing for the Sacrament of Confirmation.

Sponsor's Prayer: This is a special prayer for each stage of the program. You may decide to say it just once at the start of each new phase or to pray it daily.

Sponsor's Reflection: This reflection touches upon general themes and topics that your candidate will be learning in this phase of the program. It can also help you consider where you are on your own faith journey. You may discover that, as your candidate grows in faith, you will draw closer to Christ and the Church as well.

Conversation Starters: The suggested conversations on the following pages provide a launching pad for fruitful discussion between you and your candidate. Feel free to use them as-is or to put them into your own words if you prefer. Several possible discussions are suggested for each phase. Choose one, and then think about and prepare your own answers before you talk to your candidate. This will make the conversation more natural. Reading from the book during your time together might turn your candidate off.

Your goal should be to draw out your candidate's thoughts and feelings about what he or she is learning and experiencing. Be sure to *listen* and ask follow-up questions! If you find yourself stumped by a question and need help locating the answer, consult the *Catechism of the Catholic Church* or ask your parish priest.

① "The Way" – On the Road to Discovering Christ

It would be best to have this first conversation with your candidate after he or she has completed Lesson 6, "Why be Catholic?"

The topics your candidate will explore in this phase include the following:

Lesson 1: "Why am I here?" *(An Introduction to* Chosen*)*

Lesson 2: "What makes me happy?" *(Discovering God as the Source)*

Lesson 3: "What's your story, God?" *(A Look at Salvation History)*

Lesson 4: "How do I know God is real?" *(Understanding Divine Revelation)*

Lesson 5: "Who is Jesus?" *(The Person and Mission of Christ)*

Lesson 6: "Why be Catholic?" *(Discovering the Church Jesus Founded)*

Sponsor's Prayer

Lord Jesus, sometimes my heart is restless, and I am distracted by worldly desires and cares. When I pursue things that are contrary to your will for my life, I feel unsatisfied. I am restless because I have not turned to you wholeheartedly. Help me to know that you are the source and fulfillment of my desires and the healer of my brokenness. Empower me, Jesus, to be a living witness to you, especially to the candidate you have entrusted to me. May my heart, being more fully united with you, be a beacon of your love to all the people in my life. Amen.

Preparing for Sunday

Visit usccb.org, and click on the interactive calendar to locate the assigned readings for a particular Sunday or weekday Mass. Share this link with your candidate via Facebook, Twitter, email, or text message. You could also simply print out the Scripture readings. Discuss the readings before Mass with your candidate so you can both prepare to enter into the liturgy fully.

Sponsor's Reflection

"What do you want?" What an awkward and invasive conversation starter. Imagine that a stranger, without preamble, looked at you and asked, "What do you want?" What if the tone indicated this question was not simply about your immediate desires, but was an audacious inquiry into your deepest, most private longings?

In John's Gospel, Jesus' first words to his disciples embody this very question: "What are you looking for?" As you can imagine, the disciples do not know how to answer. So they answer with another question: "Rabbi, where are you staying?" Jesus replies, "Come and see."

Three lines of conversation have never been more loaded. The disciples clearly do not even know how to express the longing of their hearts. They are not seeking *something* as much as *someone*. Like us, though, they just cannot identify the source of their restlessness.

All of us have restless hearts. In this journey toward Confirmation, both you and your candidate are being called to follow Jesus and to discover more deeply the answer to the question, "What do you want?" This first phase of *Chosen* ("The Way") will break down barriers to belief and then introduce the basic gospel message. Your candidate will come to see how Christ, through his Church, fulfills the deepest longings of our hearts.

At this point of the program, your mission is to help your candidate delve into questions that will lead to informal but purposeful conversation.

If you are not be able to meet face to face because of distance or time constraints, consider using Skype, email, a phone call, or social media to connect with your candidate. While the activities suggested below could be done via any of these forms, consider the special value of hearing a voice and seeing a face, especially when dealing with the more personal questions in this section.

Conversation Starters

Discussion #1

Consider the following questions to address with your candidate. You do not have to use them all. Just pick your favorites. Then use them as starting points to discuss the Faith

Break the Ice

To open this or any discussion with your candidate, start with simple conversation. Spend a few moments chatting about your candidate's interests, such as sports, music, or hobbies or about life in general. Sharing some of yourself can help the conversation flow more naturally.

and your candidate's spiritual journey. Listen carefully and to ask follow-up questions. Also, share your own thoughts and ideas as the conversation progresses (being careful not to dominate).

- What makes you happy?

- What was the happiest day of your life?

- What makes you unhappy or gets in the way of your happiness?

- What are some ways you could "prove" that God exists?

- When have you felt close to God?

- Have you ever felt disconnected, or even abandoned, by God?

- What are some of the questions you have about God?

- How would you describe Jesus to someone who has never heard of him?

- How has your understanding of Jesus and your relationship with him changed as you have gotten older?

- What are some misconceptions you think people have about Jesus?

- What makes the Catholic Church different and unique compared to other churches?

- What are some good reasons to be Catholic?

Discussion #2

Email, text, or mail your candidate five of these faith-related, thought-provoking fill-in-the-blank statements. Ask him or her to finish the statements with a word or phrase, and tell them you will do the same. Choose from the following, or make up your own. Then share your answers with one another and elaborate on your responses.

- I live for _____.
- I was happiest when _____.
- God is _____.
- God is not _____.
- I feel close to God when _____.
- Jesus is _____.
- The Church is _____.

Discussion #3

Ask your candidate what saint name he or she plans to choose for Confirmation, and why. If your candidate is keeping his or her baptismal name or simply has not chosen a saint yet, talk together about your favorite saints—and why you like them.

Another Way to Think About It

The *Catechism of the Catholic Church* calls the sacraments "'powers that come forth' from the body of Christ" (CCC 1116).[10]

_____

[10] St. Leo the Great, *Sermo*. 74, 2: PL. 54, 398.

2 "The Truth" – Encountering the Light of Christ

It would be best to have your second conversation after your candidate has completed Lesson 14: "Why have I been Chosen?"

The topics your candidate will explore in this phase include the following:

Lesson 7: "Where am I going?" *(A Look at the Four Last Things)*

Lesson 8: "How do I get there?" *(The Power and Purpose of the Sacraments)*

Lesson 9: "When did my journey begin?" *(Baptism, Your Initiation into God's Family)*

Lesson 10: "Why tell my sins to a priest?" *(The Healing Power of Confession)*

Lesson 11: "How does God help when it hurts?" *(Anointing of the Sick and Redemptive Suffering)*

Lesson 12: "Who is the Holy Spirit?" *(Meeting the Third Person of the Trinity)*

Lesson 13: "What does the Holy Spirit do for me?" *(Gifts for the Journey)*

Lesson 14: "Why have I been *Chosen*?" *(Sealed and Sent in Confirmation)*

Lesson 15: "Why do I have to go to Mass?" *(Encountering Jesus in the Eucharist)*

Lesson 16: "What does it mean to say, 'I do'?" *(Marriage, a Sign of God's Love)*

Lesson 17: "Who's calling?" *(Holy Orders and Vocational Discernment)*

Sponsor's Prayer

Lord Jesus, you are not merely the teacher of truth, you *are* the Truth that brings order to everything. When I am tempted to settle for half-truths, distortions, or outright lies, draw me into the light of your presence so that I might seek you with my whole heart. Help me to experience the Church as a sanctuary of timeless truth in the midst of an ever-changing world. Through the Holy Spirit, give me the courage to speak and live the truth in love, even when it is difficult, inconvenient, or dangerous. Help me to grow in love and knowledge of truth. Through your grace, may I always be a witness to my candidate of the guiding presence of the Holy Spirit. Amen.

Sponsor's Reflection

"What is truth?" The Gospel of John records a rather startling conversation between the Roman governor, Pontius Pilate, and Jesus on Good Friday. Jesus, already flogged, crowned with thorns, and mocked, faces a death sentence. Caught between condemning a seemingly innocent man or potentially inciting a riot, Pilate interrogates Jesus. Confronting a severely beaten and bloodied Christ, Pilate asks him, "What is truth?" (John 18:38).

Little did Pilate know that the full answer to the question, "What is truth?" was the person standing before him. Jesus Christ is Truth, and he reveals, in himself, the fullness of truth about who God is and who we are.

During this time of preparation, your candidate is being encouraged to enter into a deeper relationship with Christ and his Church. This phase of the *Chosen* program, "The Truth," begins with the question of eternity, which is the goal of the Christian life. Our "end game" is not the here and now, but heaven.

When we reflect on death, judgment, heaven, and hell, we can develop an entirely new vision of our everyday world. If heaven is real, and if our eternal salvation is truly at stake, doesn't this reality change everything? How can we attain heaven and avoid hell? Jesus clearly taught that *he alone* is the source of salvation (see John 14:6). But how do we receive the eternal life he has won for us?

According to Jesus, the path of salvation is through the Church. Of course, this does not mean that only Catholics can be saved. It means that "all salvation comes from Christ the Head through the Church which is his Body" (CCC 846). Jesus has tied his saving work to the Church he founded.

Jesus promised that the "gates of hell" will never prevail against his Church, and he gave his apostles the power to govern it (see Matthew 16:18), a power and authority they passed on to their successors, the bishops. The Lord commanded the apostles to baptize and preach the gospel, thus establishing the sacramental life of the Church (see Matthew 28:19). Our most profound encounters with God are in the sacraments—outward signs of the spiritual realities given to us by Jesus himself.

The sacraments give us the grace they signify (see CCC 1131). The water of Baptism symbolizes our passing through death and coming out of the tomb with Jesus; in Baptism, we are actually reborn into the life of God's grace. Through the words of prayer and the anointing with sacred chrism in Confirmation, we receive a true anointing of the Holy Spirit. In the Eucharist, under the forms of bread and wine, we receive the true Body and Blood, Soul and Divinity of Jesus. In the Sacrament of Reconciliation, we receive true forgiveness of our sins by confessing them and receiving absolution from the priest who acts *in persona Christi*.

Understanding that the sacraments are true encounters with Christ is essential to the Christian life, so exploring the power of the sacraments with your candidate can have a profound impact on him or her—as can your example of praying and participating in the sacramental life of the Church.

Conversation Starters

Discussion #1

Have a heart-to-heart conversation with your candidate about death and eternity. Many of the Church's teachings only make sense from the perspective of eternal life. Here are some questions to explore together:

- The *Catechism* states, "Those who die in God's grace and friendship and are perfectly purified live for ever with Christ. They are like God for ever, for they 'see him as he is,' face to face" (CCC 1023).[11] What does it mean to see God "face to face"?[12]

- What is the significance of believing in the resurrection of the body?

---

[11]   *1 John* 3:2; cf. *1 Corinthians* 13:12; *Revelation* 22:4

[12]   See "What is the meaning of life?" on page 50 and "Is there life after death?" on page 53.

- Read Matthew 25:31-46 together. What does the analogy of the sheep and goats imply about judgment and eternity?

Discussion #2

Discuss the Sacrament of Reconciliation with your candidate, and then go to Confession together at your parish (or a neighboring parish). Share about your experience over a quick snack or dessert.[13]

Discussion #3

As your candidate progresses in *Chosen*, discuss what the Sacrament of Confirmation is and what it accomplishes. Ask your candidate to share what Confirmation means to him or her. Discuss that Confirmation is more than a ceremony, noting the following points (see CCC 1302–1305):

- Confirmation completes the Christian initiation begun at Baptism.

- Confirmation is a sealing with and an outpouring of the Holy Spirit.

- Confirmation empowers us for Christian life and service to God and the Church.

Discussion #4

Vocation **is an essential word for Christian life**. Everyone is called by God to a particular *state in life*—to marriage, religious life (i.e., as a brother or sister in a religious order), Holy Orders (i.e., as a priest or deacon), or the single life. We need to discern

---

[13] See "Why do I need to confess my sins to a priest?" on page 58.

this calling with serious reflection and prayer. As a sponsor, you can be deeply influential in establishing a healthy vision of discernment and openness to God's calling. You are also in a position to guide your candidate as his or her process of discernment continues in the future. Here are a few suggestions to open a conversation about discernment:

- Talk about your own state in life and how you discerned God was calling you to it. If you are still in the process of discernment yourself, talk about how it is going and where you feel God is calling you.

- Ask your candidate about any role models he or she has for each state of life. Share a few of your own.

- Ask your candidate if he or she has any fears or apprehensions about discernment. Be aware that this may be a sensitive topic because of personal history—divorced parents, a fear of religious life, a doubtful attitude about the future, or other issues. Listen thoughtfully to your candidate on these matters.

- Pray together for discernment. A simple way of entrusting the future to God is to ask the Blessed Mother for her intercession by praying a Hail Mary.

3 "The Life" – Choosing Ultimate Happiness

It would be best to have this third conversation with your candidate after he or she has completed Lesson 21: "Do I have what it takes?"

The topics your candidate will explore in this phase of the *Chosen* program include the following:

Lesson 18: "Are you talking to me?" *(Getting to Know God Through Prayer)*

Lesson 19: "Who is Mary?" *(Meeting the Mother of God – and Your Heavenly Family)*

Lesson 20: "What would Jesus do?" *(The Beatitudes as a Path to True Happiness)*

Lesson 21: "Do I have what it takes?" *(Building Virtue – Your Spiritual Workout)*

Lesson 22: "Why wait?" *(God's Plan for Love and Sex)*

Lesson 23: "How do I build the kindgom?" *(Saying "Yes" to the Mission of Christ and His Church)*

Lesson 24: "Where do I go from here?" *(The Journey Continues)*

Service Suggestion

Invite your candidate to a donation challenge. Choose a charitable cause, such as a local food bank or crisis pregnancy center and commit to match the amount of money your candidate donates.

Sponsor's Prayer

Lord of life, you made me to share in your own life, and you desire for me to be with you for eternity. Help me to be truly open to life, especially the new life of grace that you constantly offer me. May I never settle for being comfortable, but always seek the greatness to which you call me. Like your first disciples, may I always follow you and witness to my candidate and to all the world the great joy of knowing you, the source of all life. Amen.

Sponsor's Reflection

"I came that they may have life, and have it abundantly" (John 10:10). Jesus came not to limit our fun, take away our joy, or make us slaves to rules; he came to bring us the fullness of life. He lived, died, and rose from the dead so we can be free and fully alive. In our hearts, we often do not see the life of faith in this way. We can fall into the false notion that rules exist only as a means for us to earn God's approval. We fear that following Jesus seriously might mean the loss of our true identity and freedom.

We may resist, in the words of St. John Paul II, "opening wide the doors of our hearts to Christ" because this might require us to change our current lifestyle. We are often lured away from Christ by a world that is quick to settle for instant thrills and comfortable habits, rather than the abundant life promised by Jesus.

Pope Benedict XVI spoke about this: "The ways of the Lord are not easy, but we were not created for an easy life, but for great things ..."[14]

---

[14] Address of His Holiness Benedict XVI to the German pilgrims who had come to Rome for the Inauguration Ceremony of the Pontificate, April 25, 2005.

Your candidate, and perhaps the whole culture, may be strongly tempted to settle for a comfortable life, rather than the great and abundant life that true discipleship entails. Living for Christ—the greatest adventure—may indeed entail sacrifice, but only in this adventure can we find the abundance we deeply desire.

Think back to Jesus' question noted earlier ("The Way"): *"What do you want?"* At any given moment, we might crave comfort and entertainment, but no pleasure brings with it total satisfaction. No comfort ultimately satisfies. No entertainment ultimately fulfills. Our indisputable human experience is that we want more than anything this world can offer.

Jesus calls us to himself. His words to the first disciples were simply, "Come, and you will see (John 1:39)." And what did they see? They saw a radical challenge to the status quo and to everything they had always known. They witnessed demons being cast out, lepers being healed, the deaf hearing, the blind seeing, and the lame walking. They saw Jesus give his own life and then conquer death in his resurrection; they witnessed his ascension. They saw Jesus' own life and mission carried out in their own lives, effected by an outpouring of the Holy Spirit. They found what their hearts had always been seeking.

Soul Food

As the date of Confirmation nears, plan a special meal with your candidate to create a sense of the significance of this event. Consider choosing a nicer restaurant and perhaps even dress up for the occasion. This will help to signify that Confirmation is both special and serious.

In this phase of *Chosen*, your candidate is exploring the call to authentic discipleship. A life of discipleship is rooted in prayer, a hard habit to learn in our noisy and distracted world. We turn to the lives of Mary and the saints as the models of the fullness of life in Christian discipleship. Your candidate will be looking more deeply at what daily life in Christ means and will be looking ahead to Christian life after Confirmation.

St. Irenaeus said, "The glory of God is the human person fully alive." In this third conversation, explore with your candidate how he or she can be more fully alive in prayer and discipleship.

Conversation Starters

Discussion #1
Check in. Take your candidate out for dinner and ask how he or she is doing. If you are drawing a blank, you can ask simple things like, "How is life?" "What is your favorite class?" "Are your friends good to you?" "Any drama at school weighing you down?" "What are your latest dreams for your life?" "How are you doing with living your faith?" or "How is life at home?"

Discussion #2
Pick a common act of service to perform with your candidate. If you live nearby, you may want to join him or her. If not, choose a similar activity that you can each do in your respective locations. For example, you can each serve at a local food bank or soup kitchen or visit a nursing home. After you have completed your acts of service, consider the following questions:

- What does it mean that we *find ourselves* when we *give ourselves away*?

- What does it mean to be "poor in spirit" (as in the Beatitudes)?

- St. Teresa of Avila says, "Christ has no body but yours, no hands, no feet on earth but yours." How can we be Jesus' hands?

- What is a particular type of service to which you feel called?

Discussion #3

Have a heart-to-heart talk about how we are expected to live as Christians after Confirmation. Emphasize that Confirmation is not an end to learning and living the Faith, but rather an empowerment to do so in a fuller, more mature way. Explain that you will be available in the future to listen and to answer questions, and that you will pray for him or her every day for the rest of your life. (That will be extremely meaningful to your candidate.)

Legacy of Faith

Write an encouraging "real" letter to your candidate that expresses how much you appreciate him or her. In an age of abbreviated, disposable communication, a handwritten letter can become a lifelong treasure for your candidate to re-read over the years.

Mystagogy: Life After Confirmation

While it is important and highly recommended for you to have at *least* one follow-up conversation with your candidate after his or her Confirmation, this fourth phase should be an ongoing dialogue!

Sponsor's Prayer

Holy Spirit, open my heart to the same newness of life that you breathed upon the apostles at Pentecost. Help me to live and move in the fullness of your gifts and to never waver from my commitment to live the life I have found in Christ or from full participation in the life of the Church, Christ's body. May I never settle for a half-hearted life of faith. Lead me into the abundant life Christ won for me. Fill me with the grace and wisdom to lead my candidate toward a life of peace, happiness, and joy, which can be found only in you.

Sponsor's Reflection

What happens after Confirmation matters. Many who receive the sacrament simply disappear from the life of the Church. When they leave the Faith, they miss out on the fullness that God calls them to in this life, and they put their eternal salvation at risk. Sadly, cultural apathy leads many away from the Church, and the Church needs *your* help as a sponsor to ensure that your candidate's renewed life in the Spirit takes root. Encourage him or her to attend Mass every Sunday and to go to Confession regularly. Offer ongoing guidance so that your candidate's intellectual grasp of the Faith will continue to grow.

The ancient Church observed a period of fifty days after Easter during which the newly baptized and confirmed received further instruction and formation. This formation period was known as *mystagogy*, meaning "leading into the mysteries." Baptism and Confirmation were seen not as the "finish lines," but as the "starting gates" of the life of faith, and *mystagogy* helped the newly initiated Christian understand how to live this faith fully. *Mystagogy* remains part of the Church's formal sacramental formation today, as part of the Rite of Christian Initiation of Adults (RCIA).

While your parish may or may not have actual sessions for the newly confirmed, *mystagogy* is important in nurturing a new life of faith, and as a sponsor, you can have an important impact. Here are some specific ideas for continuing to support your candidate after Confirmation.

Conversation Starters

Discussion #1

For a few months, call or text your newly confirmed young Catholic every week with a reminder to attend Sunday Mass. Invite the teen to go with you, perhaps with an invitation to go out to breakfast or dinner afterward. If possible, study the readings together or discuss the homily after Mass. If your candidate was already devoted to weekly Mass prior to Confirmation, touch base periodically to ask if he or she has started attending a youth group or is finding other ways to live out the grace of Confirmation. This simple gesture of accountability can be very helpful in establishing good habits.

Discussion #2

Encourage your candidate to go to Confession at least once a month. Some find it helpful to establish a habit of going to Confession on the first Saturday of every month or some other day. Join your candidate, if possible, or text him or her a simple reminder. Establishing accountability here can benefit both of you.

Discussion #3

Make a date to meet one month after Confirmation for a deeper discussion of the life of faith. Here are some suggested topics:

- How is your prayer life developing? What are you doing to keep in contact with God on a daily basis?

- How will you continue to deepen your knowledge of the Faith? (Perhaps you could suggest a spiritual book to read and discuss together.[15])

- What areas of the Catholic Faith do you want to learn more about?

- How are you staying connected to the parish community (or youth group)?

- What are you doing to witness for Christ at your school?

---

[15] See page 73; "Additional Reading/Gift Ideas."

Celebrate a Feast Day

Look up the feast day of your candidate's chosen patron saint. Use this date as an "anniversary" to do something special with your candidate. You could also observe the feast day by sending your candidate a "Happy Feast Day." card or message via Facebook, text, or Twitter.

Part 3

FAQ

Top Ten
Catholic Questions

"Lord, I do not seek to penetrate your depths because
I cannot even remotely approach them with my own
intellect. However, I wish to understand, at least to a
certain point, your truth, which my heart believes and
loves. Indeed, I do not seek to understand in order to
believe, but I believe in order to understand."

–St. Anselm

This section will assist you in discussions with your candidate by providing answers to common questions about Catholic doctrine and the life of faith.

1. *What is the meaning of life?*

This is the central question to which every human person seeks an answer—at least subconsciously. Thankfully, God has not hidden the answer from us: We exist to know and love God, to live in his love by serving him and others, and, ultimately, to be united to God in love forever in heaven. We can succeed at everything else, but if we fail at holiness, we fail at the reason for our existence. If we succeed at holiness, we can have a purpose, peace, and love that nothing in this world can take away. Success at holiness is not just success at what you have done, but at who you have become.

People have tried to live for a thousand other things, but none of what the world offers ultimately satisfies us. We can find countless examples of those who have an abundance of wealth, intelligence, athletic skill, or artistic prowess, but none of these, in themselves, satisfies the deepest longing of our hearts. Instead, we find ourselves thinking: *There must be something more.*

Gift Idea

Make a prayer journal for your candidate. You can use any sort of notebook or journal and customize it by inscribing spiritual quotes and Scripture verses on the blank pages for your candidate to discover as he or she uses it.

Consider again the observation of Pope Benedict XVI: **"The world offers you comfort, but you were not made for comfort, you were made for greatness."** The world's philosophies focus on making us comfortable, on satisfying ourselves; and this is precisely why they all fail. The human heart is not made to be fulfilled by mere comfort.

As St. Augustine famously said, our hearts are restless until they rest in God. St. John Paul II observed, "It is Jesus that you seek when you dream of happiness; he is waiting for you when nothing else you find satisfies you; he is the beauty to which you are so attracted; it is he who provoked you with that thirst for fullness that will not let you settle for compromise; it is he who urges you to shed the masks of a false life."[16]

2. If God is good and all-powerful, why does he allow so much suffering and evil in the world?

Suffering is a difficult and inevitable part of life. It can cause us to collapse into fear, rage, or despair. The psalmist wrote: "... my only friend is darkness" (Psalm 88). Unfortunately, sentiments like this do not make good sympathy cards.

When tragedy strikes, many respond by saying that God must have a good reason, that everything is within God's providence, or that he is allowing suffering to make us stronger. While all these things are true, the words can ring hollow for those overwhelmed by grief or loss. Suffering can indeed lead to unforeseen goods or contribute to character growth—but that knowledge is not very comforting when a child is stricken with cancer.

[16] John Paul II, World Youth Day, Rome, August 19, 2000.

Service Suggestion

Invite your candidate to a "works of mercy" challenge. Together, review the works of mercy described in CCC 2447. Challenge one another to find opportunities to perform each of them. Discuss your experiences afterward.

Some believe all suffering in a person's life is God's punishment for his or her sins—and yet this explanation also falls short. In the Old Testament, when Job endures countless sufferings, his friends claim he must have offended God and brought the suffering upon himself. In the end, God makes it clear that Job's friends are all wrong (see Job 42:7-17).

The story of Job contains profound insight into the nature of suffering. After chapters of questioning God, Job is reduced to silence. God does not attempt to answer all of Job's questions one by one, but simply makes it clear that he is God, and Job is not (see Job 38:1–42:6). In the end, the only answer Job gets to the problem of pain ... is the person of God. This answer becomes ever clearer on Good Friday.

Look at a crucifix. Take a moment to pause, look, and reflect. The crucifix is a brutal display. Why is such violence hanging on our walls? Around our necks? In our hands, with the rosary?

The cross is the greatest sign of love in history. It reveals that God would die not only to redeem us, but to be with us in our experiences of darkness. *Through the cross and the Resurrection, God presents us, not with a theoretical answer to the problem of evil, but with his own transforming life.* We have the promise and hope of the empty tomb on Easter Sunday. We suffer, but we suffer in hope.

3. Is there life after death? What about heaven and hell?

In his earthly ministry, Jesus frequently spoke of the reality of heaven. Because he knew it would be hard for us to wrap our brains around the concept of eternity, he used words we could understand when describing heaven: "In my father's house there are many rooms." He told his disciples, "If it were not so, would I have told you that I go to prepare a place for you?" (John 14:2).

Then, when he was done *teaching* us about life after death, he *showed* us that reality. Through his bodily resurrection, Christ showed us that death does not have the final word.

So what is heaven like? St. Paul advises us to remember, "No eye has seen, nor ear heard, nor the heart of man conceived, what God has prepared for those who love him" (1 Corinthians 2:9). God is the source of all that is good. Every true joy we experience in this life is like a ray of light coming from the sun and touching us. In heaven, we will experience the source of all goodness directly as we behold God face to face. This is called the "beatific vision." Hell, conversely, is where people are separated from God, and, as a result, from the light of truth, beauty, and goodness that flows from him.

Jesus Christ is the only way to get to heaven. He said so himself: "I am the way, the truth, and the life; no one comes to the Father, but by me" (John 14:6). This means that everyone, even non-Christians (who can make it to heaven "in a way only known by God"), only get there because of the redeeming work of Jesus

Christ (see CCC 847). No one can earn entrance into heaven by being a "good person." This does not mean we should not strive to be good. It means we cannot "earn" heaven—even by our best efforts. It has been opened to us by the passion, death, and resurrection of Christ and is given to us as a gift. If we live in conformity with his will and die in his grace, we will be able to receive that gift.

But how could a loving God consign people to an everlasting hell? The simple answer is that God does not want anyone to go to hell, nor does he "send" anyone there. Unrepentant sinners freely choose hell by refusing God's grace. God never ceases to love us, but he has given us freedom so we can love him; we are free to refuse his love. A great Christian apologist, C.S. Lewis, writes: "There are only two kinds of people in the end; those who say to God, 'Thy will be done,' and those to whom God says, in the end, '*Thy* will be done.'"[17]

Both heaven and hell are real. Where we spend eternity is our choice. This reality should bear enormous influence on how we choose to live.

---

[17]   C.S. Lewis, *The Great Divorce* (New York: HarperCollins Publishers, 2001), 75.

4. *Why should I be Catholic?*

Jesus Christ, the second Person of the Trinity, founded a visible, structured Church and promised to remain with his Church until the end of time (see Matthew 28:20). He chose twelve men, the apostles, to lead that Church by his own authority. These Twelve in turn handed on that authority to the bishops, their successors. Adding further structure to his Church, Jesus placed Peter over the apostles and gave him and his successors, the popes, a special grace to teach firmly, faithfully, and without error in matters of faith and morals (see Matthew 16:18).[18] Furthermore, Jesus instituted and entrusted the *sacraments* to the Church to dispense the grace he won for us.

While elements of truth can be found in other faiths, and especially in other non-Catholic, Christian churches, the fullness of truth is found in the God-man, Jesus Christ, and in the Church he founded.

It is important to note that the Church is the *guardian* of truth, not the *source* of truth. The Church cannot change its teachings because these truths are not its to change. The Catholic Church is God's idea. Perhaps the best evidence of this is that the Church has survived these past 2,000 years despite the sinfulness of its members, scandals, and widespread persecution by many kings and governments throughout history. If the Church were merely a human institution, it would be nothing more than a distant memory by now.

While speaking to and engaging those of other faiths, we should celebrate the things we share in common, while always remaining ready to explain what we believe. As requirements

---

[18] See *Lumen Gentium* 12; CCC 889.

of faith, Catholics should be committed to loving everyone, regardless of religious belief, and to striving for genuine unity and dialogue among all faiths, especially with our non-Catholic, Christian brothers and sisters (because more unites than divides us). But, while interreligious dialogue, shared outreach to the community, and ecumenical prayer are important, we must be clear and unapologetic about what makes Catholic identity distinct.

5. Why do I have to go to Mass every Sunday?

"OK," someone may ask, "I get that I should pray to God, but why do I have to go to Mass? Can I just honor God in my own way?" The answer: Of course you can worship God "in your own way" and pray whenever you feel like it. However, God *commands us* to worship him in a communal and Eucharistic way—at Mass.

Jesus called us to this kind of worship at the Last Supper, when he commanded, "Do this in remembrance of me" (Luke 22:19). God also commanded us to, "Remember the Sabbath day, to keep it holy" (Exodus 20:8). In keeping with Christ's resurrection, the Church celebrates the Sabbath on Sunday, which for Christians is a "little Easter."

At Mass, we worship God as a community, pray together for our needs, collect gifts for the needs of the community, ask for forgiveness from each other, and make peace with others in the community. The "together" part is important. We get together with family and friends to celebrate events such as Baptisms, weddings, graduations, concerts, and the Super Bowl. Why shouldn't we celebrate together the most important event of all?

At Mass, we also fulfill Christ's command that our worship be Eucharistic. As the *Catechism* says, "The Sunday celebration of the Lord's Day and his Eucharist is at the heart of the Church's life" (CCC 2177). At every Mass, we participate in Calvary in a profound way when we receive the Eucharist. If we believe Jesus is truly present in the Eucharist, what could be more important than being united with him every Sunday in a way that cannot happen anywhere else?

Beautiful music and an inspiring homily are good for us, but the primary purpose of attending Mass is to unite ourselves to Christ. In this union, our worship is transformed into something infinitely profound and eternally powerful.

In addition to attending Mass every Sunday, we are also required to attend Mass on six *holy days of obligation*: the solemnity of Mary, the Mother of God (January 1); Ascension Thursday (transferred to the following Sunday in most U.S. dioceses); the Assumption of Mary (August 15); All Saints Day (November 1); the Immaculate Conception (December 8); and Christmas.

Think of it this way. In the ordinary routine of life, there are many occasions that we are obligated to celebrate because of their importance, such as birthdays and wedding anniversaries. The more important your relationship with the person honored in the celebration, the more important your participation is and the greater disappointment your absence would cause. There is no more important person than God, and we honor him when we attend Mass.

6. Why do I need to confess my sins to a priest?

In John's Gospel, the resurrected Christ walked into the room where the apostles were gathered, breathed on them, and said, "If you forgive the sins of any, they are forgiven; if you retain the sins of any, they are retained" (John 20:23). In this act, Jesus instituted the Sacrament of Reconciliation, giving the apostles the power to forgive sins with his authority. So, when you confess your sins, you are not confessing your sins to the priest, but to Jesus.

Confessing is not always easy. Visits to doctors and dentists are often uncomfortable, awkward, and sometimes embarrassing. Yet these feelings do not usually keep us from going at the early signs of a problem. We deal with whatever embarrassment or discomfort we feel in order to receive healing. When our souls are in need of care, then, is it not reasonable that we should seek healing—even if it feels uncomfortable?

Yet, it can be more obvious when we need to see a doctor than when we need to go to Confession. Mortal sins are a rejection of God's grace. When we choose to sin seriously, we choose to reject God, and the wound to the soul is mortal because we lose sanctifying grace—the grace we need to enter heaven.

Even small sins can have big consequences. If we neglect to seek treatment for flu, it can develop into pneumonia and put our lives at risk. If we neglect the healing of our sinful souls, even for minor sins, we can develop a weakness for mortal sin.[19]

---

[19] For a sin to be mortal, three conditions must be met:

- The act is a "grave matter," i.e., a serious violation of God's law.
- It is chosen with full knowledge that it is a serious violation.
- It is *freely* chosen (i.e., with "full consent" of the will). One cannot commit a mortal sin "by accident" or by being forced.

What if you are not sure whether you have committed a mortal sin? When in doubt, go to Confession. Not going would be like ignoring chest pains until you pass out (or die) from a heart attack. So take good care of your spiritual health. Confession is yet another way Jesus, through the ministry of his Church, conveys spiritual realities through tangible, sacramental encounters.

7. *How can we believe that the pope is infallible? After all, he is just a man.*

Yes, the pope is indeed "just a man," but since the days of Abraham, Isaac, and Moses, God has entrusted amazing tasks to fragile people. Jesus left us an organized religion. He chose twelve apostles to lead the Church, and one of them, Peter, he made the "head" of the apostles. The authority of the apostles to govern the Church has been passed down to the bishops and the pope of today.

In Matthew 16:18-19, Jesus told Peter, the first pope, "And I tell you, you are Peter and on this rock I will build my church, and the powers of death shall not prevail against it. I will give you the keys of the kingdom of heaven, and whatever you bind on earth shall be bound in heaven, and whatever you loose on earth shall be loosed in heaven." In biblical language, keys are a clear symbol of authority (see Isaiah 22:22).

So, what does the pope's teaching authority over the Church mean? First, let us be clear on what infallibility is *not*:

- The pope is not infallible in political or social affairs.

- Infallibility does not mean the pope is free from sin, as Peter's denials of Christ demonstrate.

- The pope's personal theological opinions, expressed in books or articles, are not infallible. (Popes John Paul II and Benedict XVI both wrote a number of books and shared many theological reflections during their pontificates.)

Infallibility refers to the inability of the Church's Magisterium to make an error when teaching definitively on matters of faith or morality.[20] It can be exercised by the pope alone, when he issues a defined teaching *ex cathedra* ("from the chair") or by the world's bishops gathered with the pope in an ecumenical council.

8.   *Do I have to believe everything the Church teaches?*

Although we do not have to agree with every policy set by our local parish or every pastoral decision of our Church leaders, being a follower of the Lord Jesus entails accepting the essential teachings of the Church he founded.

If you are Catholic, you believe that Jesus is God and that he founded a Church to teach the truth. The Church's teaching authority rests on the authority Jesus gave it, particularly in matters of faith and morals. Given that the Church teaches with Christ's own authority, it is reasonable to assume that the Church is correct even when we disagree with a particular teaching.

---

[20]   See *Lumen Gentium* 12.

We live in an age that prizes individual judgment and opinion over received wisdom. It is an era of distrust for "authority." But when we are talking about things that have been revealed by God, it makes sense to soften our hearts to *receive* a teaching from an authority.

The Church's teachings are not random assertions of the pope and bishops given without any explanation or historical context. Everything the Church teaches is based on divine revelation, is reasonable, has been verified by the experience of credible witnesses, and has been studied and explained by some of the greatest minds in history. Often, when a particular teaching seems irrational to someone, it is because he or she has not taken the time to study the reasons behind the teaching.

Of course, it is not always easy to follow the teachings of Jesus and his Church. The Church's mission is to help "earth rise to heaven." So we should not be surprised when our earthly inclinations sometimes conflict with God's laws. In our weakness, we might recoil from "difficult" truths that require sacrifice to live out. With God's grace, though, we can come to believe and live the hard truths of the gospel, trusting his mercy as we strive for holiness.

9. Why must we save sex for marriage?

Many people mistakenly think the Church gives boundaries to sexual behavior out of a negative or puritanical view of sex. In reality, the Church's view is that sex is so incredibly good, so sacred, that we must do everything we can to ensure that it is lived as God created it to be lived.

Your candidate may ask, "OK, but if two people truly love each other, why must they be married to have sex?"

Many acts of our bodies function as a "language" and have universally recognized meanings. For example, we all know that a smile communicates something totally different than crying does. If these gestures had no standard, universal meaning, they would be meaningless. Furthermore, body language is "truthful" only when it corresponds to reality. For example, if I am deeply depressed but do not want anyone to know, what do I do? I *fake* a smile. This smile communicates something that is not true.

The meaning of sex is rooted in its very nature: It communicates the existence of a mutual self-gift that is free, total, and faithful (exclusive) and that has the power to be life-giving (fruitful). Marriage is the *only* context where sex can be truthful, because marriage is the *only* context where this degree of relationship exists. Sexual intimacy before marriage communicates a degree of relationship that does not yet exist.

The Church's teaching on sexuality and marriage can be summarized this way: *Tell the truth with your body.* While a couple is dating or engaged, the spousal relationship does not yet exist, so their body language must not communicate that it does.

There are numerous medical and psychological advantages to being truthful with one's body in sexual matters. Premarital sex increases the risk of disease, painful breakups, teen depression, and ruined reputations. It greatly increases the chance of future divorce and hardship because of unintended pregnancy. (These are all well-documented risks.)

But the most important advantage of being truthful with one's body is that it allows the person to pursue authentic love, which puts what is good for someone else before what he or she might want from that person. And an act that is not good for someone else is the opposite of love, no matter how it might feel on an emotional level. As Scripture tells us, real love always "rejoices in the right" (1 Corinthians 13:6).

10. How can I know God's will for my life?

Seeking and discovering God's will for our lives is known as *discernment*. The process of discernment involves prayer and openness to the people and experiences God brings into our lives, all of which can help us find the path to which he is calling us. Some people expect God's direction to be in the form of mystical visions or miraculous signs. Even the saints only received such phenomena on rare occasions (if at all). Typically, God communicates with us in a way that is very fitting for body-soul creatures—through our experiences and our ability to reason.

When we face a big decision or are at a crossroads, planning for the future, or trying to determine how to respond to a situation, we need to discern God's will in the midst of conflicting voices and desires. Our decisions have consequences not only for our own lives but for others' lives as well. As a unique and "unrepeatable" human person, each of us has a place in the body of Christ that *only* we can fulfill.

St. Catherine of Siena summarizes the significance of personal vocation: "If you are what you should be, you will set the whole world ablaze!" Discerning God's plan for you begins with some practical considerations that may not seem especially extraordinary, yet are fundamental. Even though we may wish for more sensational divine intervention, we still encounter God most often in the poverty of a manger and under the appearance of the plainness of bread and wine—in the basics.

- *Remain open to hearing God by remaining in a state of grace.* Sin can block God's voice in our hearts and minds. Like static on a phone line, sin makes hearing God increasingly difficult, distorting his voice and ultimately deafening us to it altogether. In contrast, the grace we receive through the sacraments, especially the Eucharist and Reconciliation, helps make our "connection" to God clear.

- *Fulfill the daily responsibilities of your current vocation with love.* Whatever God ultimately has planned for you, one thing is certain: He wills that you give yourself in love wherever you are *now.* Our vocation, although it unfolds and develops over the course of our lives, does not begin at some point in the future. It begins now, and we must always strive to make a gift of ourselves wherever we find ourselves.

- *Pray often.* Prayer is conversation with God. All relationships depend on communication, and this is especially true of the spiritual life. St. Paul advises us to "pray without ceasing ... for this is the will of God" (1 Thessalonians 5:17-18, NAB). God calls us all to be in relationship with him. Everything else—including the specific vocation meant for us—flows from this one certainty. Jesus himself promises that if we concentrate on seeking first the kingdom of God, "all these things shall be [ours] as well" (Matthew 6:33).

- *Talk to people.* You cannot discern your life's direction in a vacuum. Ask questions of people who are doing something you think you might be interested in doing.

Part 4

Additional Resources

"God calls man first. Man may forget his Creator
or hide far from his face; he may run after idols or
accuse the deity of having abandoned him; yet the
living and true God tirelessly calls each person to
that mysterious encounter known as prayer."

–CCC 2567

Catholic Prayers

Apostles' Creed

I believe in God,
the Father almighty,
Creator of heaven and earth,
and in Jesus Christ, his only Son, our Lord,
who was conceived by the Holy Spirit,
born of the Virgin Mary,
suffered under Pontius Pilate,
was crucified, died and was buried.
He descended into hell;
on the third day he rose again from the dead;
he ascended into heaven, and is seated
at the right hand of God the Father almighty;
from there he will come to judge the living and the dead.
I believe in the Holy Spirit,
the holy catholic Church,
the communion of saints,
the forgiveness of sins,
the resurrection of the body,
and life everlasting. Amen.

Our Father

Our Father,
who art in heaven,
hallowed be thy name;
thy kingdom come,
thy will be done, on earth as it is in heaven.
Give us this day our daily bread,
and forgive us our trespasses

as we forgive those who trespass against us;
and lead us not into temptation,
but deliver us from evil. Amen.

Hail Mary

Hail Mary, full of grace, the Lord is with thee.
Blessed art thou among women,
and blessed is the fruit of thy womb, Jesus.
Holy Mary, Mother of God,
pray for us sinners,
now and at the hour of our death. Amen.

Glory Be

Glory be to the Father,
and to the Son,
and to the Holy Spirit.
As it was in the beginning,
is now, and ever shall be,
world without end. Amen.

Hail, Holy Queen (Salve Regina)

Hail, Holy Queen, Mother of mercy,
our life, our sweetness, and our hope.
To thee do we cry, poor banished children of Eve;
to thee do we send up our sighs,
mourning and weeping in this valley of tears.
Turn, then, most gracious advocate,
thine eyes of mercy toward us,
and after this, our exile,
show unto us the blessed fruit of thy womb, Jesus.
O clement, O loving, O sweet Virgin Mary.

Pray for us, O Holy Mother of God …

That we may be made worthy of the promises of Christ. Amen.

Memorare

Remember, O most gracious Virgin Mary, that never was it known that anyone who fled to thy protection, implored thy help, or sought thy intercession was left unaided. Inspired with this confidence, I fly unto thee, O Virgin of virgins, my Mother; to thee do I come, before thee I stand, sinful and sorrowful. O Mother of the Word Incarnate, despise not my petitions, but in thy mercy, hear and answer me. Amen.

How to Pray the Rosary

Begin by praying the Apostles' Creed (on the crucifix), an Our Father (on the first bead), three Hail Marys (on the first set of three beads), and a Glory Be (on the space).

Next, pray the five decades, each comprised of an Our Father, ten Hail Marys, and a Glory Be. Each decade is assigned a particular mystery on which to reflect (see "Mysteries of the Rosary" immediately following).

Conclude by praying the Hail, Holy Queen and the following prayer:

O God, whose only begotten Son, by his life, death, and resurrection, has purchased for us the rewards of eternal life, grant, we beseech thee, that meditating upon these mysteries of the most holy Rosary of the Blessed Virgin Mary, we may imitate what they contain and obtain what they promise, through the same Christ our Lord. Amen.

Mysteries of the Rosary

The Joyful Mysteries
(traditionally prayed on Mondays and Saturdays)

- The Annunciation

- The Visitation

- The Nativity

- The Presentation

- The Finding of Jesus in the Temple

The Sorrowful Mysteries
(traditionally prayed on Tuesdays and Fridays)

- The Agony in the Garden

- The Scourging at the Pillar

- The Crowning with Thorns

- The Carrying of the Cross

- The Crucifixion

The Glorious Mysteries
(traditionally prayed on Wednesdays and Sundays)

- The Resurrection

- The Ascension

- The Descent of the Holy Spirit

- The Assumption of Mary

- The Coronation of Mary

The Luminous Mysteries
(traditionally prayed on Thursdays)

- The Baptism of Jesus

- The Wedding at Cana

- The Proclamation of the Kingdom

- The Transfiguration

- The Institution of the Eucharist

The Divine Mercy Chaplet

Using a rosary, begin with the Sign of the Cross, one Our Father, one Hail Mary, and the Apostles' Creed.

On each Our Father bead, pray:

Eternal Father, I offer you the Body and Blood, Soul and Divinity of your dearly beloved Son, our Lord, Jesus Christ, in atonement for our sins and those of the whole world.

On each Hail Mary bead, pray:

For the sake of his sorrowful passion, have mercy on us and on the whole world.

Repeat above prayers on each decade.

End by praying three times:

Holy God, Holy Mighty One, Holy Immortal One, have mercy on us and on the whole world.

Additional Reading/Gift Ideas

The following books would make great gifts for your candidate:*

- *Did Adam & Eve Have Belly Buttons? And 199 other questions from Catholic teenagers* by Matthew Pinto

- *Did Jesus Have a Last Name? And 199 other questions from Catholic teenagers* by Matthew Pinto and Jason Evert

- *Do I Have to Go? 101 Questions About the Mass, the Eucharist, and Your Spiritual Life* by Matthew Pinto and Chris Stefanick

- *Theology of His Body/Theology of Her Body* (2 books, 1 volume) by Jason Evert

---

* This list also appears in the *Chosen* Parent's Guide, so you may want to check to be sure you are not duplicating gifts.

About the Authors

Aimee and Colin MacIver teach theology at Saint Scholastica Academy in Covington, Louisiana, where Colin serves as the religion department chair and campus ministry coordinator. In addition to teaching in Catholic high schools, they have also served in various youth ministries for nearly ten years. The MacIvers reside in the New Orleans area with their young son.